BOOM For The Baby Boomers

Judi Jaques

I DEDICATE THIS BOOK TO ALL BABY BOOMERS BUT
ESPECIALLY TO BOTH MY BROTHERS DOUG AND JIM
AND THEIR WIVES DIANNE AND LESLEY

May we all grow older, wiser and more profitable
together love sis.

CONTENTS

CONTENTS

ACKNOWLEDGMENTS

I would like to acknowledge my husband Peter for his patience in putting up with me in getting this book written.

I also acknowledge my daughter Ammie, she is my constant inspiration.

I need to also acknowledge my two mentors, Brett McFall and Steven Essa, guys without the both of you and your inspirational encouragement this book would never have been completed and my world has changed for the better. How can I ever say it enough, thank you.

CHAPTER 1
HOW GRANDPARENTS CAN
EARN A PASSIVE INCOME

How many Grandparents are there in our world?
While many of you can cleverly go to look this statistic up via Google or similar internet source I just want to firstly start my book series with the Genre of Baby Boomers.
I believe that this generation was and still remains the largest populace of the world and in many circumstances the leaders of many things. Unfortunately in the consumer world we currently live in the Baby Boomer generation have led the trends for example Clarks School shoes or just Clarks shoes in general. After the war when babies were booming, small comfy shoes were in demand, this was just one in a long line of consumer needs that have been met over the past half a dozen decades or so.
What has this got to do with Grandparents making a passive income you ask? As the Baby Boomer generation have grown, not only consumerism but technology has grown as well. Also we are now becoming known as an ageing population, we are all for the most part living longer. Now as you know the longer one lives the more needs of the person and again I feel our generation will lead a way a new way

to earn money – good money using the internet as a tool.

Today's Internet is a far cry from when computers first appeared on the scene in the 60's and 70's. Today we all need to embrace this new technology as it is with the assistance of this that we will be able to provide not only for ourselves but for our ageing parents and for our children and grandchildren. You see many of the Baby Boomer generation are not only the carers of their ageing parents but in many circumstances the carers or full time guardians of their grandchildren, either through tragic accident or other means.

The financial pressures can be enormous not to mention the emotional trauma associated with all of this. Now here we are in 2013 and we need to find a way, after the GFC (Global Financial Crises) many have lost their superannuation

OR LOST A GOOD CHUNK OF IT!

This brings me back to now. How many of you have ever heard the expression, hind sight is the best sight you will ever have? Well I believe the vast majority of us have not only heard this but also statements like, I wish I had... If only... If I had my time over I would have...

Well what if I was to tell you right now the next sentence could change your life forever! Now I am sure you would agree that is a very powerful statement. Yes? Action speaks louder than words!

Having said this I invite you now to come on a money making journey with me that when you take ACTION, you will change your life forever.

There are several ways "we" can make money using the internet and social media as tools to assist us in this goal.

The following are simply just ways that you can choose and or combine to make money on the internet.

Writing EBooks and selling them online.

Making a WEBINAR, invite firstly friends and relatives to your webinar.

Do this until you feel comfortable then the sky is the limit. You can interview an "expert" every week and make a new webinar each time. Write up 10 interesting questions to ask the expert and with the expert's answers you now have 10 chapters of an eBook on that topic. It could be a person you know who is an avid gardener, full of many tips. Here is an example of ten questions you can ask?

Question 1

What is...?

Question 2

What is so good about......?

Question 3

Can you give us a little bit of background about how

you got involved in....?

Question 4

What is the best way to get started?

Question 5

How long does it really take to become proficient at...?

Question 6

If you had one secret to give about …… what would it be?

Question 7

What are some of the common problems that people experience in …?

Question 8

Can you provide a real life example of someone who has followed your advice?

Question 9

Where can people find more information about...?

Question 10?

How can people contact you?

Do Joint venture deals with this person say 60% to them -40% to you for every eBook you sell?

Make a series of CD's and or DVD's of your EBooks to sell now you suddenly have 4 different mediums to sell.

Google is my new best friend and I am sure many of you (in my vintage) have already discovered that you can search for just about anything at the push of a few buttons. However, if you are anything like me you soon discover there are a few - gaps or holes in carrying out certain functions or instructions along the way.
This is where I come in. You see I have discovered that by doing this searching on the internet and to make some money really is not as easy as "they" being the experts are saying. True?!
I have literally spent many dollars-$47 for this bit of information, $27 for that bit of information, $97 to

join this membership and all in the end leading to nothing. I mean no money for my return. This by the way is only a snippet of what I have spent over the last 6 years.
I then discovered a way that actually does work and I am getting money weekly now and this is how:
Affiliates- What is an affiliate? Someone who has close association with. The English dictionary says:" to associate oneself; be intimately united in action or interest. "

You can become an affiliate for as many companies as possible which is FREE to do, and once you have accounts with for example CLICKBANK, then the world is your oyster as you then promote other people's products on your own pertaining WEBSITE and or FACEBOOK page. The following are other examples of companies I have become an affiliate with:

Adsense

Ebay Partner Network

Commission Junction

Chitika

Overstock

Linkshare

Amazon Associates

Join different groups in social media as in pick on your hobbies first for example Golf. In the facebook search bar type in golf and there are literally hundreds of different groups, check them out, ask if you can join their group, interact by writing posts (comments) within that group about the topic they are currently talking. After a day start by telling them about your EBook or CD or DVD or WEBINAR, you will be amazed at how many "friends" you will attract. Now I place "friends" in inverted commas because these people are really not your friends, right? These are people that are just interested in your topic of conversation loosely called friends. This is good because in the Social Media world the more "friends" you have, this equates to more traffic i.e. people and the more traffic the more exposure for your products and the more exposure the more money you will make. Does this make sense to you?

There is so much more I want to share with you but for now I have to state this.

In the next section I feel I am connecting with 2 different types of folk. Let me explain, for the computer savvy people at this point please go and make a cup of tea or coffee as I am directing this next section to the complete novice who knows there is money to be made using the internet but no idea how to get started?

CHAPTER 2
IT ALL STARTS FROM THE RESEARCH

In chapter one I gave you a bit of an overview but now we are going to pull it all apart and get stuck into it, let's begin.

There are 3 things you need to make money using the internet.
1/ A product
2/ A website and or Facebook customized page
3/ As much traffic as possible

Now let's look at these 3 things in more depth to create a better more understandable situation.
1/ Product
Now as people say Rome was not built in a day, neither was the internet. You need to research the marketplace to find out what is selling and work with that knowledge. OK you have hobbies and interests, you want to have a go at selling garden tools, you love gardening and you think this is the go. WAIT! Before you start you need to know, is this what people will buy? You see there are 5 things that make up the qualities that are the most important for you to have a saleable product and they are:

1. Product Reviews and / or testimonials

2. Unique Selling Position (USP)
3. Market Leadership
4. Ease of Purchase
5. Professional Appearance / quality website and
shopping cart experience

Part of finding your product requires research.

Firstly, get a free account with **GOOGLE** base. This
will allow you to utilize all sorts of tools including the
KEYWORD EXTERNAL TOOL. This is a great tool,
however like any tool you need to set it up to suit
your needs this is how:

a/ Go to http://googleeasysearch.com, sign you're
your Google account. Once the tool is opened you
need to change the parameters for searching.
You need to have a look at the boxes on the left
hand side and the default box broad needs to be
unticked then the box "phrase" needs to be ticked.
Then under the box in the centre where you will type
your term to be researched you need to tick all
countries, leave language at English, leave desktop
and laptop devices, change to global monthly
searches instead of local monthly searches and add
another filter competition and click on low and
medium box not on high. Once you have done this
you then type in the term or words you want to
research. I have inserted here screen shots of
exactly what to do in order to search for your
interest, to see if you have a market.
http://youtu.be/cuYwP47qC1I
Now this is exciting as you now have a term or

otherwise known as a market or niche. For this exercise it is - Garden Rake Types - now you know through your research and the first search you scroll down the page for a term that closely relates to your words you have typed in you are looking for approx 1600 to 3500 in this first search. Once you have found that then you click on the term in the first column and a drop down box appears click onto the Google Search and another window appears with your new term in the browser box. You then add inverted commas before and after this in the browser box and when you click on search again your number needs to be approx 20,000 – 35,000 people globally, (around the world) are searching for this exact item.

2/ Build A Website and/or a Facebook customized Page

Great, the next thing you need to do is build a website and or a customized facebook page, now using this researched title as the title for your website or facebook page. The title will be Garden Rake Types, now together let me assist you in navigating your way through building a customized facebook page. Why facebook you ask? Good question. Currently as from 30/04/2013, 835,525,280 people around the world use Facebook per month. Just think about that for one moment. What are the chances of your facebook page with the availability of instant traffic (people) more likely to get an audience of up to 20,000 per month? I think very good chance.

Now what I am going to share with you here is out there for you to discover however I believe most people like me don't have a clue where to start so I have a simple video I made here showing you exactly how to build a facebook page and then to add Affiliate links and customize your page. For any of the links I quote all you have to do is type the link into the browser of your internet connection.

http://youtu.be/z50WY52FAug Creating a customized Facebook Page

http://youtu.be/1SinIE9q9Ig Creating a link on your website for your customized Facebook Page

Now I am going to show you the process needed to obtain a product to sell on your page. This again is totally FREE.

http://youtu.be/katEI9eAY4I finding a hot product through ebay

Now we are going to add this link of this product into our page

http://youtu.be/e-Jcp8tnchI Creating a link to your website

Congratulations! You now have a customized facebook page with a link to a product that if sold will attract to you 75%. This will occur 24 hours a day 7 days a week. You can be looking after your grandchildren or doing the many tasks I know "we" baby boomer do. We are avid multi-taskers and we get things done.

3/TRAFFIC. This is a major key to earning money on the internet.

Traffic is the life blood of any internet business. You can have the best looking website with beautiful images and great features. If no one knows about it what good is it? Traffic is a term we give to people who visit your website.

None of the afore mentioned will amount to any income without traffic. How does that song go?.....

"People who need people are the luckiest people in the world".... Shirley Bassey and later Barbra Streisand never sung such truer words.

How to Generate Targeted Site Traffic without Search Engines

"If search engines were never invented or they ceased to exist tomorrow,
 how would you build traffic to your website in a search less world?"

That's the first question each of us search-addicted webmasters should
ask ourselves every morning. While search is really hard to beat in terms
of cost-of-traffic and its targeting, don't leave these other options out of your Web Promotion Playbook. Learn how to thrive on the Internet without having to worry about the unpredictable algorithm changes of search engine algorithms and you've created a truly defensible audience.

In no particular order, each of these methods of engaging the Internet
will deliver to you targeted, monetizable web traffic:

1. Blogging. There are a hundred good reasons as to why you should
 be blogging, but in terms of building a web audience, the two best reasons are
A) It gives you near immediate time-to-market with your message and
B) It's a great way to put a face behind your message. Popular blog services like Technorati can deliver great traffic. If we take our search engine blinders off, blog search engines are now reaching high enough adoption rates to send over great traffic, too. Ok, search blinders back on. Don't forget to be an active and valuable commenter on the blogs of other key influencers in your business.

2. Podcasting. Webinars. I don't have any specific stats on podcasting,
but just ask yourself, "Do I or anybody I know listen to podcasts?"
I'm betting the answer is, "Yes!", and the number is higher than it was
a few years ago. Like blogging, Podcasting is a great way to control your
message and bring it to market quickly.

3. Link buying. Search engines turn up their noses at link buying, but
I have been buying links long before they were used to juice link popularity scoring. A good link can deliver tons of targeted traffic. Some Wikipedia links deliver way more benefit from their traffic than they ever did from their link authority. See: Text Link Ads.

4. TV Buys. It turns out TV time really isn't that expensive in local markets. Check out Spotrunner. You can buy great air time for a whole lot less than you probably expected.

5. Web Directories. This is how the Internet used to be organized and the
genesis of Yahoo. While most fly-by-night directories won't ever send you enough traffic to merit the fee, take a look at Aviva Directory's List of the Strongest Directories. Work your way down this list and you'll see targeted traffic.

6. Ad Networks. One of the things I always try to do is buy ad inventory on any pages that rank above me. Many of the most trafficked sites on the
Internet sell ad space or let ad network services like AdBrite or IndustryBrains resell the space. There is gold in some of them hills!

7. Online Forums. Like web directories, online forums can trace their history back to the earliest days of Internet traffic. But like blogging, it's a great way to personalize your interaction with your audience while building traffic.

8. Social Media. Aside from search engines, this is the motherload of traffic. Whether you're building a large Myspace and Facebook presence, establishing yourself as a thought leader on linked in, or seeing your content promoted on Digg, Netscape, and Reddit...this is probably the largest yield of any audience building effort

9. Email List Rentals. This is a huge driver of traffic in the B2B and direct marketing worlds. If you can get the right cross section of traffic in a list, it's very profitable. Just make sure the provider of the list is in compliance with all the laws regarding this activity.

10. Webinars/Video. Webinars just might be the hottest audience building
tool in the B2B world. Like podcasting, you can really go the extra mile in personalizing the message and interaction with your audience.
Video communities like YouTube are a great source of traffic. What the
audience lacks in buying intent, it makes up for in the ability to take your content viral.

11. Online Press Releases. Maybe the oldest and most resilient of the
traditional media promotional tools, the online version is also effective. You'd be surprised how many news outlets rely on newswires. Take advantage of that through online press release agencies like PRWeb.com.

12. PR Firm. A PR firm won't pull a rabbit out of a hat, but the good ones are amazingly good at creating inertia behind your product or service. Their Rolodexes will make it easier to do everything else on this list.

13. Event Media Sponsorships. If you are a news blogger...or your site can
 pass as a news site...this is an amazing source of traffic and branding that most online publishers have overlooked. Just about every major conference,

seminar series, or symposium is looking for media sponsorships. You'll get a valuable link on the event website plus you can market to event goers with other materials in the registration bags, booths at the show, and email blasts. The results of doing this in the B2B world are nothing short of amazing.

14. Sponsored Reviews. There are a million bloggers out there who are
looking for topics to write about and get paid. The concept of the sponsored review was designed by firms like ReviewMe and PayPerPost to solve this problem. Many of the Technorati Top 100 blogs can send you thousands of visitors.

15. Syndicate Your Content. There are thousands of other businesses out
there who are unable or unwilling to create their own content. For example, many Fortune 500's display third-party content to aid their audience in buying decisions. There are also a ton of article sites with active audiences and/or good traffic. Make sure you require a link back to your original source, though. You know...to establish canonicalization for those search engines we are trying to ignore.

16. Find funny you tube videos with no links or videos with a lot of traffic and no weblink. Contact the owner; offer them $100 to place your domain at the bottom of the video. You never know until you ask! Just remember that every one person you get as a customer is in fact equal to one dollar per month! 20,000 people = 20,000 dollars.

CHAPTER 3
WHAT IS AN AFFILIATE

In chapter 1 we touched on the term Affiliates- What is an affiliate? Someone who has close association with. The English dictionary says:" to associate oneself; be intimately united in action or interest. "

Now let's explore this whole new world of Affiliates more closely. This enables you to start earning money without a product, even without a website which I have been saying, you need to make money with! Pleased do not get confused by this. I do not know your situation so if you need to make money fast then this is how. You sign up with a company called Clickbank. You sign up as an affiliate not a vendor. Affiliate is FREE. Then once signed up you go to the marketplace, choose a category and then search for a product that will give you a minimum of 50% commission and also look at the gravity the higher the better. This gravity means that more of those products are selling weekly. Once you like a product you can even write an email to the owner of the product if you wish you then click on Promote and another box opens up. Now I strongly suggest you highlight and copy the text link onto a word doc in your files and also highlight and copy the html code link and paste under the above text link in your word doc. This will save you a lot of time down the track. Next you open up another tab in your browser and type in tiny URL this will bring up a free site that will convert your link to a smaller one that is disguised meaning the hackers in the world out there will not be able to hack into your link in any way. Highlight and paste this tiny URL to your word doc as well. Now you have 3 links there and you label them or title them the name of the product.

The next thing I need you to do is open up your facebook account and if you have not already you need to create a page, which will be a business page for this product or relating to this product for example take my term I researched, garden rake types. I make a page on Vegetable Garden Planning, also on Garden Rake Types and I can then add a post and drop in my tinyurls link. As people visit and click on my link they may buy. Now it is all a formula. At the moment every subscriber you have is equal to one dollar per month, you get 20,000 you receive on an average $20,000 per month.

OK? So this is a quick way to earn money as an affiliate but the more sustainable way is exactly as I said before, research a product, term, build a website, get traffic = convert>make money. So now we will work through the Affiliate processes a bit more. By definition **Affiliate Marketing** is a set of practices used by websites to drive traffic to other websites. Let me put it to you this way. The smaller websites direct traffic by various means IE: links, pay-per-click deals, performance based commission set ups, and outsourcing content such as blogs and through these means or practices directs traffic to the larger website.

I thought to get involved in this **Affiliate Marketing** more deeply I had better 'bone up' or gain some knowledge on subjects like SEO (search engine optimization) and simple content and development of content. But you know what? If you pick up on an idea that 'tickles your fancy', then I have learnt to go for it. I mean really GO FOR IT. Don't stop until you conquer what it is that you are seeking. Now you need to have an affiliate account with as many companies as you can and I will include the list of companies in the next chapter that I am affiliated with but there are many more you will be able to discover for yourself.

The main point I am trying to get across to you here is that companies today around the world are paying good money to everyday folk like us to have a website and or a facebook page or as well a Twitter account and advertise links. So I am asking you now to research again but this time any large company you can think of and way at the bottom of the page there is usually a small print word saying affiliate. Click on read the terms and conditions, if you like the %commission then go for it. What are you waiting for? I hear you, what if it doesn't work? Well what if it does? Now is not the time for self doubt and procrastination. Remember my saying that I live by and these 10 tiny 2 letter words, *If It Is To Be It Is Up To Me.*

Look at companies like Pepsi, Merrell shoes, K-Mart and many, many others. At the bottom of the sites they sometimes say join our partner program which when you click on is in fact and affiliate program. So do not hold back, get out there on the net the internet and become an affiliate to as many companies as you can. One final tip from me, make sure you have a note book or exercise book of some kind and write in it every company you sign with the user id or email that you sign up with and the password used for each company. This is very important as this book will become your "Book Of Knowledge".

I personally have a foolscap sized ring bound alphabetically tabbed book that is my book of knowledge that I have placed into my will for my children. This is how valuable it is.

CHAPTER 4
MY TOP TEN AFFILIATE
COMPANIES AND HOW TO
JOIN THEM.

No beating around the bush here my Top 10 Affiliate companies I am a member of are:

Adsense
Amazon Associate
Commission Junction
Chitika
E-Bay Partner Network
Clickbank
Linkshare
Overstock
Webfire
Pepsi

First is Adsense. Have you ever noticed the Ads on the right hand side of websites that are usually in blue? Google ads or Adsense ads, this is a very easy account to obtain and implement onto your websites.
Go to https://www.google.com/adsense
I know this sounds simple and it is but I have been approached by many people to say they cannot get into Adsense. I think this is because

many people have a Google account of some kind and you either connect your existing Google account or remember your separate email addresses. Another tip I bought a piece of software several years ago now called http://www.roboform.com as this great software remembers all my codes and passwords, however this does not replace my book of knowledge because if the internet were to shut down or lose signal or computer fails you still have your written copy that enables you to enter all details to the different sites so you can continue your business.

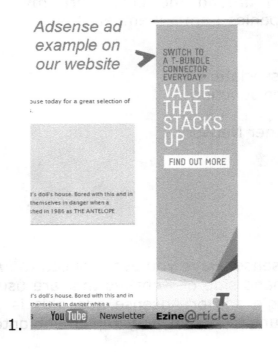

1.

So this is an example of an Adsense Ad on one of my sites. This is a picture ad we also have text ads the choice is yours. The next Affiliate company we will talk about is Amazon Associate. You need to enter https://affiliate-program.amazon.com There are many products within Amazon

and just like your research in chapter 1 you are able to research the popular selling items here in whatever category that is here. For example I purchased 3 x ebooks

Through Amazon on line costing me a total of $27, now I went through my affiliate link and I got paid $24 from Amazon for making the sale. So $3 for 3 books is not bad I also found out my links work.

Once you have been approved for a Amazon Associates account then remember to keep the login details written in a book.

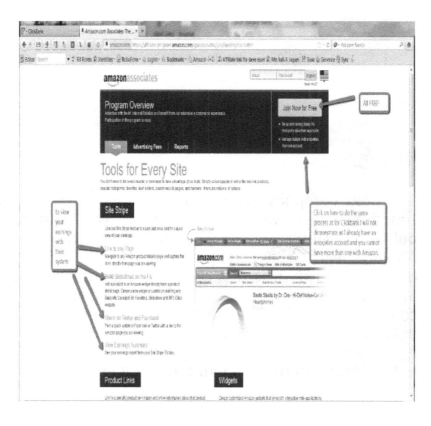

The next company we will talk about is Commission Junction. Now with this company you join as a publisher. Don't let the processors of becoming an Affiliate with this company turn you off, it is definitely worth it as this company then allows you to automatically be affiliated with literally hundreds of companies that register with them. I get paid 30-50 dollars a day with this company. Go to http://www.cj.com/get-started-now
the following page is what you will see.

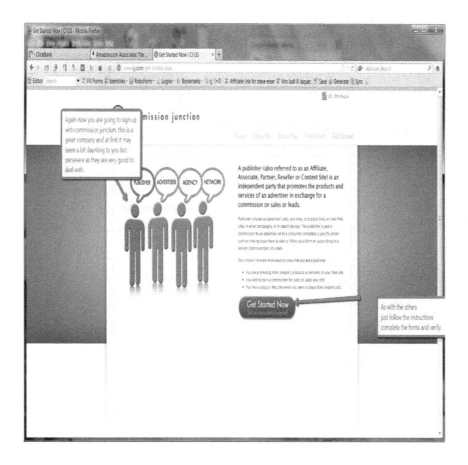

Just follow the instructions and remember you are a publisher with this firm.

You should already have a ClickBank account, the next company is Chitika. This company also call you a publisher, you need to go to: https://publishers.chitika.com/ or **http://tinyurl.com/bvpwrhg**

This is a great company who pays well and gives

great data feedback.

So now I want to cover E-Bay partner Network. I will print in a slide here but first just let me say that this is the big one guys and gals! It took me 3 months to get this account but my income increased by 70%. E-Bay Partner network is not the same as the regular Ebay. Around the world today there are only 400,000 Ebay Partner network affiliates, of which I am one. There are millions of Ebay users around the world. Now the main thing you need to do before you submit a site to E-Bay is make sure there are no ads on the site, great content on the site and interaction with people of at least 50 comments which you reply to on your site. Starting out this maybe difficult but get your family, friends to help with commenting.

The following slide is the sign in window.

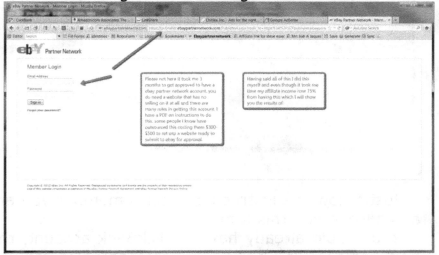

NOW I SUGGEST YOU READ AND WATCH ALL DATA AND TUTORIALS BEFORE YOU GO AHEAD HERE

I know people who have outsourced this to an overseas company in order to get through the requirement process and paid $300 to get a site made for the purpose and failed to get approval. So I urge you to persevere once again if I can do it you should be able to.

Once you have this account approved you can then go ahead and load all of your sites to Ebay Partner Network and away you go. Next we are going to look at used domain names.

CHAPTER 5
WHY HAVE A USED DOMAIN?

Firstly, what is a domain name? Why do you have to have one? These are 2 great questions and I will attempt to answer them now in regular talk not computer talk!!

Now, when you build yourself a website what is it that you want to do? Many people just like to have a blog which is a modern day term for a journal on the internet. In order for your blog or website to be seen it has to have two things. The first thing is a domain, this is often referred to as a link between your website to the internet. In my limited knowledge no one seems to remember these domain names they simply type into the search bar what it is they are looking for, the words, and these words become keywords, words that people use to find a website or information. The second thing you need to have your website seen on the internet is a host and I will talk in depth on this topic in the next chapter.

So a domain, you need to pay money for a domain name and there are many companies you can deal with. Please take the time to look up a couple or more before you purchase a domain name. Certainly you can register a domain name that you want, for example if you are going to sell all things for the caring of a dog then you might want to register the domain All things for dogs or as a domain it would look like this: http://allthingsfordogs.com or you can choose .net or .org but do not choose .info as they do not rank well with search engines. I on the other hand search for used domain names, because, the main thing you will need for your website in order to make any money is traffic so you may as well start from the beginning and try to get traffic straight away. Used domains can come with thousands of backlinks and of course a backlinks is a link pointing to that domain name, it does not matter that the site was owned by someone else, that traffic is gold. If you create a domain as in the dogs example you are starting from scratch and in doing so it will take up to a year to get traffic and credibility to your site. A used domain does need to be checked out as far as pornography and sex. Make sure the used domain has not been involved in those areas and you are safe to proceed. All of my 300 sites came with backlinks and I used either Crazy Domains.com or Go Daddy.com to purchase all of my domains.

Both these companies are very easy to deal with and very cheap. You can even get bulk discounts and specials from time to time. I tended to purchase when the 75% off sales were on. Again the domain does not have to have the same name as what your site will be. One of my sites for example is http://alrakhie.com now this site is all about postcards and the collection and buying and selling of postcards around the world. It is a very popular site and came with 5000 backlinks, it cost me a total of $11 which included the registration for 2 years. Bargain! It earns approx $50-$100 a week. Remember this is just one site, I have 300 of them, so when you add up a bit here a bit there it is quite a sizeable income.

So now you understand the importance of a domain

name and the benefits of a used domain name. Another example that I have where after the research I was looking for something along the lines of exercise for the elderly. I bought http://granintraining.com the site is named Exercise for the Elderly. This was a double bonus as the domain name relates to the topic but honestly this does not need to happen if at all to be successful.

I will now add in here a slide shot of the GoDaddy site and of a couple of the sites of mine for you to see but you are most welcome to look on the internet and see all this as well.

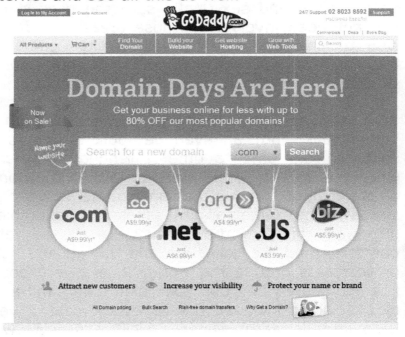

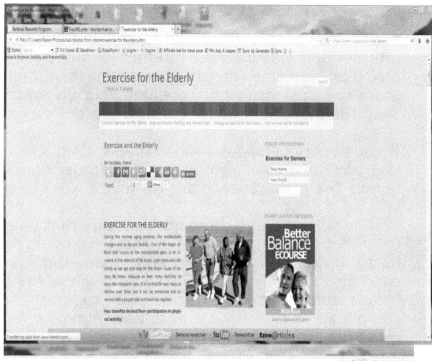

Your domain name or web address is more than your Internet address, it's your Internet identity, your online brand name. It puts your business on the map of today's business world, opening your business to over 100 million Internet users worldwide.

If you're serious about your business, then it is vital that you have your own easy to remember domain name. The main reasons are twofold:

No one will take any company seriously that has their Website hosted by one of these free Web page hosts. It doesn't say a lot for a company that can't even afford to pay for their own Web space You will have a domain name that is relevant to your company and is much easier to remember for future reference. My domain name is "yahoo.com". Now imagine that it is freespacehost.com/uk/business/yahoo". Which one is easier to remember? What makes a good domain name? The name of your company is always a good choice. If your company name is rather long and hard to remember, then choose something easy to remember and associates with your product or service.

3 Cruel Facts About Domain Name Registration.

Don't Misspell. Why? You can't reverse domain registration — once you register your domain name, you can't change it anymore... no matter what you do.

Although most domain registrars do offer a 5-day refund policy, it's a case-by-case basis. Usually you're entitled a refund for a misspelled domain name, provided you highlight to the company within 5 days upon your registration with them, but it's not an entitlement to all scenarios as they need to guard against scam practice.

Hence, you should always painstakingly ensure and verify the absolute accuracy of your domain name before you punch the 'Check Out' button. This will save you trouble and money.

2 Auto or Manual Renewal

I had a friend who has always been uncertain about whether his online business will work out or not. Unconfident, he sets the domain renewal to manual mode because he doesn't want to end up paying more if he suddenly shuts down his website for some reason.

As such, he has to personally go inside his domain account to renew year after year.

One fine year, while he was so busy with renovating his new house, his domain was due for renewal. And he had not been checking his inbox for months (his domain registrar has actually sent him several renewal notices). So, when he returned to his site after the renovation has done up to 70%, he found his website was gone!

He's no longer the domain holder. He wound up having to brainstorm for another domain name and perform domain pointing and lots of url redirects for his new domain name.

In view of this, I suggest that you register your domain name for a year first and set it to auto if you're not sure whether you're going to use it year after year. Setting it to manual renewal can be risky unless you know very well that you're giving up on this domain name soon.

3 Register Now or Never

Once you've found the right domain name that hasn't been taken up by anyone yet, grab it now!

Statistics have shown that more than 5.61 million domain names are being registered worldwide each day (i.e. over 65 domain names registered per second) with no signs of slowing down, so if you don't register now, it'll get "stolen" faster than you blink your eyes.

CHAPTER 6
HOSTING

Now remember in the last chapter I said you need two things to have your blog or website seen on the internet? Well the second one is hosting. Hosting companies have sprung up all over the globe and this is a very competitive market. There are several hosting companies so I advise you to again research and do a comparison.

You do not need a lot of extras or on sells that the different companies will offer. You just need hosting. Host gator will cost as little as $7 per month, GoDaddy $6-10 per month, Crazy Domains, Crazy Sales, are just a couple of names that come to mind. Get cracking, once you have a host and a domain name you can get started. The internet world awaits you all you have to do is make a start!

Through your hosting company you can then access http://wordpress.org and get going on building your website/s. I bought my domains through GoDaddy but I will show you a screen shot of my domains on GoDaddy but I have them hosted through a company called CoolHandle.com Please I stress you need to find a company that you can easily understand and gives you all the advice to get on with what you need to do with your domains.

What does "hosting" my web address mean?
Every web address must reside on a host computer, a domain name host. Domain name hosts are connected to the Internet and use special software to translate web addresses into the numerical

addresses used by the network. When users enter your web address, the domain name host directs them to your email or Website Without it, your web address is invisible on the Internet.

Do I need to have an Internet service provider or a domain name host before I can register a web address? Contrary to popular belief, you don't. You can reserve a web address today to assure you that your name will be there for you when you are ready to use it.

When my web address expires in two years will I be able to renew it? Yes. When you are ready to renew your web address, simply go back to the registrar of the domain name and renew it.

Can I register more than one web address? Yes! You can register as many web addresses as you like.

Can I register a web address by myself? Yes! All you need is a few minutes, some basic information about yourself, your business and your credit card or PayPal account. You can simply order over the Internet.

Where can I go to register my domain name? To register your domain name, go to one of the hosting companies and fill in the form for registration. You can register one of the 675 recognized domain extensions including .com, Net, .org, as well as all country code domains and their sub-domains. Here I will list 12 excellent tools which will allow you to first search on the domain name and verify that it has not been reserved, hence making picking a domain name an easier process.

- Domainr
- Dot-o-mator
- BustAName
- Domain Tools
- Domize
- Squurl
- DomainsBot
- dnScoop
- StuckDomains
- Nameboy
- Dyyo.com
- Ajax Whois

You'll find a variety of search and suggestion tools from within the list above all with an assortment of features so that, hopefully, you'll discover a few favourites.

The term **cloud hosting or cloud computing** consists of Internet-based computing, whereby shared resources, software and information technology resources are provided to computers and Internet servers on demand, a bit similar to the power grid that we use everyday and that we tend to take for granted, until the next power outage happens.

Cloud hosting and cloud computing is a paradigm shift following the major transition from large and costly mainframe computers to nimble and lower cost client–server technology in the early '80s. Details are abstracted from the users, who no longer have need for expertise in, or control over, the technology infrastructure "in the cloud" that supports them.

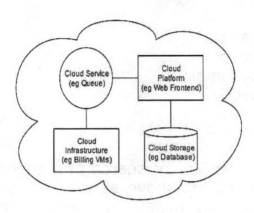

The term cloud hosting can be summarized in two short sentences: You host a Web-based application or resource somewhere on a server in a data centre. You don't need to know where that server is located or how it works, as long as it works. End of the story. Cloud hosting describes a new information delivery model for IT services based on the Internet, and it typically involves over-the-Web provisioning of dynamically scalable and often virtualized resources.

Cloud hosting is a by product and consequence of the ease-of-access to remote servers provided by the Internet. This frequently takes the form of

Internet-based software or end-user applications that people can access and use through a Web browser as if it were a program directly installed locally on their own computer.

The National Institute of Standards and Technology (NIST) provides a somewhat more objective and specific definition of cloud hosting. The term "cloud" is used as a metaphor for the Internet, based on the cloud drawing used in the past to represent a telephone network, and later to depict the Internet in computer network diagrams as an abstraction of the underlying infrastructure it represents.

Typical cloud hosting providers such as Sun Hosting deliver common business applications online that are accessed from another Web service or software like a Web browser, while the software and data are stored on servers. A key element of cloud computing is dynamic customization and the creation of a user-defined experience.

Most cloud computing infrastructures consist of services delivered through common data centres and built on servers. Clouds often appear as single points of access for consumers' computing needs. Commercial offerings are generally expected to meet quality of service (QoS) requirements of customers, and typically include service level agreements (SLAs).

Cloud computing customers do not own the physical infrastructure, instead avoiding capital expenditure by renting usage from a third-party provider such as Sun Hosting. They consume resources as a service and pay only for resources that they use. Many cloud-computing offerings employ the utility computing model, which is analogous to how traditional utility services such as electricity are consumed, where as others bill on a subscription basis.

Sharing perishable and intangible computing power among multiple tenants can improve utilization rates, as servers are not unnecessarily left idle, which can reduce costs significantly while increasing the speed of application development. A side-effect of this approach is that overall computer usage rises dramatically, as customers do not have to engineer for peak load limits. Additionally, increased high-speed bandwidth makes it possible to receive the same data and at the same time.

The cloud is becoming increasingly associated with small and medium enterprises (SMEs) as in many cases they cannot justify or afford the large capital expenditure of traditional IT resources. SMEs also typically have less existing infrastructure, less bureaucracy, more flexibility and smaller capital budgets for purchasing in-house technology. Similarly, SMEs in emerging markets are typically unburdened by established legacy infrastructures, thus reducing the complexity of deploying cloud solutions.

Cloud computing users avoid capital expenditure (CapEx) on hardware, software and IT services when they pay a provider only for what they use. Consumption is usually billed on a utility (resources consumed, like electricity) or subscription (time-based, like a newspaper) basis with little or no upfront cost. Other benefits of this approach are low barriers to entry, shared infrastructure and costs, low management overhead and immediate access to a much broader range of applications.

Users can usually terminate their contract at any time, thereby avoiding return on investment risk and uncertainty, and the IT services are often covered by service level agreements (SLAs).

The strategic importance of information technology is diminishing as it becomes standardized and less expensive. The cloud computing paradigm shift is similar to the displacement of electricity generators by electricity grids early in the 20th century.

Although companies might be able to save on upfront capital expenditures, they might not save much and might actually pay more for operating expenses. In situations where the capital expense would be relatively small, or where the organization has more flexibility in their capital budget than their operating budget, the cloud model might not make great economic sense.

Other factors impacting the scale of any potential cost savings include the efficiency of a company's data centre as compared to the cloud vendor's, the company's existing operating costs, the level of adoption of cloud computing and the type of functionality being hosted in the cloud.

So in summary there are many different choices when it comes to hosting even hosting in the clouds.

You do not have to know exactly how it all works you just need to have some form of hosting to move forward.

The following picture shows a small "slice" of the internet with several home computers connected to a server:

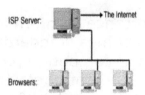

Host servers are where websites "live". Every website in the world is located on a host server somewhere. The host server's job is to store information and make it available to other servers.

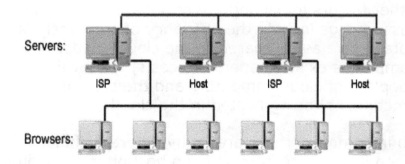

CHAPTER 7
BUILDING A WEBSITE

This seems to be the point where many people either give up, hit the wall so to speak or just feel this is too technical for me and reach a road block. You know what if you never change what you have always done then you will never see the benefits of what will happen when you do change.

Let's get started. There are many useful software user friendly suppliers out there and I do suggest initially you create a blog either through www.blogger.com or www.wordpress.com both these services are free and is a good way to get started on making your way around web page making. Also you can use this as a journal or even diary if you like of your journey to in the end making money.

Now, as far as making a website is concerned you need to be aware that I am talking about a multiple page website not a one page sales page which I refer to as a squeeze page. We will cover that in the next chapter. The following is a short list of the different software I have personally used to make websites but there are many , many others. www.wix.com
www.webstarts.com   www.weebly.com
www.webspawner.com   www.jigsy.com

www.webs.com and www.wordpress.org
Now you can check them all out for yourself as I said before there are many more pieces of software available please investigate for yourself.

I personally prefer the system of wordpress.org why? There are a few reasons, some are the ease of using the system, the variety of different templates available, the continuous updating of the system making the upkeep of my sites a much easier task. You see once you build a website there is maintenance to be carried on to keep your website current and up the top of the search engines as much as possible. Of course I invite you to discover the new world of creating websites and find your preferred method of use, life would be boring if we all were the same. My main point I want to get across to you all is that this should not be a road block to you moving forward with making money using the internet, this should be a roadway to leading onto the next step.

We all have choices to make in life, there is a saying that says you are a long time dead so in life embrace every opportunity and find a way around the not so easy stuff but just find a way. Work to live don't live to work! I have taken these words and 10 two letter words to the next level in my life, IF IT IS TO BE IT IS UP TO ME!
We all have regrets mine is I could have started this exciting journey earlier!

OK, the next thing I want to pass onto you is the fact is in order to build your own website I have given you many software links to plough in and have a go.

Realistically though, if you are a newbie and the idea of doing all of this yourself is daunting then from the outset I suggest you outsource this task. I can assist you in that endeavor – go to www.judijaques.com or here are the list of skills you will require yourself to have a go.

These skills enable you to build a website that looks good, as well as make it available for the world to see:

- *HTML* - HTML is the language that allows you to create each web page on your website. HTML stands for HyperText Markup Language and is responsible for the various elements that you see on websites - elements such as headings, paragraphs, hyperlinks, bullet lists, embedded images, embedded music/video files and more.
- *CSS* - determines how your website looks. For example, for each HTML element on your website, you can use CSS to determine its width, color, alignment, size etc. CSS stands for Cascading Style Sheets.
- *Understanding of web hosting and domain names* - to make your website available for the world to see, you need to host it on a web server. Web hosting providers make this their business, so you don't need to know all the details about web servers, firewalls etc. All you need to know is how choose the most suitable hosting provider for your website.
- *FTP* - this is only required when you need to upload your website to a web server (your hosting provider's web server). Doing this allows the world to view it. This is quite a simple thing to learn. Technically, FTP is a

protocol (it stands for File Transfer Protocol), but all you need to know is how to operate FTP software.

Optional Skills

The following skills are optional - you could easily build a website without knowing these skills. But these skills can help you make a more advanced website.

- *Image Editing* - for creating/manipulating any images you might need on your website. This is optional - you can easily build a website without any graphics, and it can look quite good too. However, if you choose to use images, you should learn how to use an image editing application such as Adobe Photoshop.
- *JavaScript* - for making your web pages more dynamic. JavaScript allows you to write programming style code that enables your website to do things such as alert messages, popup windows, status bar messages, drop-down menus, remember the user's name and much more.
- *Server-side Scripting Language* - this allows you to provide much more advanced functionality than you could achieve with just HTML/CSS/JavaScript. Server-side scripting languages are commonly used in conjunction with a database so users can interact with a website much more extensively. Any website that offers things such as blogs or forums would need to use a server-side language to allow users to post comments etc into a

database. These comments can then be read later on by other users who want to read them. Common server-side scripting languages include ColdFusion and PHP.

- *Databases/SQL* - once you need to add more advanced functionality to your website, you can use a database to store lots of data such as content. This could be either your content (articles, events, products etc), or your users' content (blogs, forums, image upload site etc).
- *Web Servers* - even if you outsource your hosting to a hosting company, you should still learn about web servers. You could install your own web server onto your own computer and have your own development hosting environment. A web server is essential if you plan on using a server side language such as PHP or ColdFusion.

I've created a series of tutorials that step you slowly through each of the skills you need to learn in order to build a website and upload it to a hosting provider. I recommend you take your time as you go through each of these.

There is a lot of information to digest, and because of this, I suggest you read these tutorials over a number of days. To help you, I've separated them into different steps in the following table. Although some of the tutorials are quite short, you may need to spend several days on others. That's fine, in fact, I recommend you take your time so that you really understand each technology.

You may even like to print this page, then tick the checkbox as you finish off each tutorial.

Step	Skill to Learn	What's Involved	Done
Essential Skills			
Step 1	Learn HTML	Create HTML documents, add hyperlinks, bullet lists, forms, tables, images, frames, and more.	
Step 2	Learn CSS	Create CSS code, specify fonts and font size, background images, adding colors, classes, IDs, float, layers, positioning, embedded style sheets, external style sheets, and more.	
Step 3	Learn about Website Hosting	How to choose a web hosting provider, domain names, use FTP software to upload your website to a hosting provider, monitoring your website, and more	

Optional Skills

Step 4	Learn about Web Graphics	Learn about web graphics software, uploading images to the web, embedding images into a web page.
Step 5	Learn JavaScript	Enabling/disabling JavaScript, JavaScript syntax, variables, functions, operators, loops, if statements, reading/writing cookies, displaying the date and time, arrays, and more
Step 6	Learn ColdFusion	Installing ColdFusion, ColdFusion syntax, "include" files, variables, if statements, loops, arrays, redirecting pages, automatically send emails from your website, debugging, error handling, uploading files to your website, writing FTP applications, charts,

and more.

Step 7	<u>Learn Databases</u>	Learn about databases, database design, how to insert data, read data and more.
Step 8	<u>Learn SQL</u>	SQL syntax, writing basic queries to read data from a database, programmatically insert/update/delete data from a database, programmatically creating a database and its objects (such as tables, indexes), count the number of records in a table, learn about SQL functions, and more. Note: This tutorial assumes a basic knowledge of how databases work.

Step 9 (optional)   Learn PHP

Many of the things you learned in the ColdFusion tutorial can also be done with PHP. In particular, this tutorial covers PHP installation, syntax, variables, if statements, arrays, loops, operators, uploading files, sending mail, and more.

Step 1 HTML Tutorial

HTML, which stands for HyperText Markup Language, is a markup language used to create web pages. The web developer uses "HTML tags" to format different parts of the document. For example, you use HTML tags to specify headings, paragraphs, lists, tables, images and much more.

HTML is a subset of Standard Generalized Markup Language (SGML) and is specified by the World Wide Web Consortium (W3C).

What do I need to create HTML?

You don't need any special equipment or software to create HTML. In fact, you probably already have everything you need. Here is what you need:

- **Computer**
- **Text or HTML editor**. Most computers already have a text editor and you can easily create HTML files using a text editor. Having said that, there are definite benefits to be gained in downloading an HTML editor.

  If you want the best HTML editor, and you don't mind paying money for it, you can't go past Adobe Dreamweaver. Dreamweaver is probably the best HTML editor available, and you can download a trial version for starters.

  If you don't have the cash to purchase an editor, you can always download a free one. Examples include SeaMonkey, Coffee Cup (Windows) and TextPad (Windows).

If you don't have an HTML editor, and you don't want to download one just now, a text editor is fine. Most computers already have a text editor. Examples of text editors include Notepad (for Windows), Pico (for Linux), or Simpletext/Text Edit/Text Wrangler (Mac).

- **Web Browser**. For example, Internet Explorer or Firefox.

Do I need to be online?

No, you do not need to be online to create web pages. You can create web pages on your local machine.

STEP 2 CSS

What does CSS stand for?

CSS stands for Cascading Style Sheets.

What is CSS?

CSS is a language that you can use to define styles against any HTML element. These styles are set using CSS *properties*. For example, you can set font properties (size, colors, style etc), background images, border styles, and much more.

Cascading Style Sheets, level 1 (CSS1) became a W3C Recommendation in December 1996. It describes the CSS language as well as a simple visual formatting model. CSS2, which became a W3C recommendation in May 1998, builds on CSS1 and adds support for media-specific style sheets (e.g.

printers and aural devices), downloadable fonts, element positioning and tables.

Advantages of CSS

- **CSS saves time**
  When most of us first learn HTML, we get taught to set the font face, size, colour, style etc every time it occurs on a page. This means we find ourselves typing (or copying & pasting) the same thing over and over again. With CSS, you only have to specify these details once for any element. CSS will automatically apply the specified styles whenever that element occurs.
- **Pages load faster**
  Less code means faster download times.
- **Easy maintenance**
  To change the style of an element, you only have to make an edit in one place.
- **Superior styles to HTML**
  CSS has a much wider array of attributes than HTML.

Disadvantages of CSS

- **Browser compatibility**
  Browsers have varying levels of compliance with Style Sheets. This means that some Style Sheet features are supported and some aren't. To confuse things more, some browser manufacturers decide to come up with their own proprietary tags.

  Fortunately, browser compatibility is becoming less of an issue as the latest browser versions are much more standards-compliant than their earlier counterparts.

Implementing CSS

There are 4 ways of implementing CSS: declare *inline*, *embed* into the head of your document, link to an *external* CSS file, *import* a CSS file.

Inline CSS

Style sheet information is applied to the **current** element. Instead of defining the style once, then applying the style against all instances of an element (say the <u><p></u> tag), you only apply the style to the instance you want the style to apply to.

Embedded CSS

You embed CSS information into an HTML document using the 'style' element. You do this by embedding the CSS information within <u><style>... </style></u> tags in the head of your document.

For example, place the following code between the <u><head>... </head></u> tags of your HTML document:

External CSS

An external style sheet is a separate file where you can declare all the styles that you want to use throughout your website. You then link to the external style sheet from all your HTML pages. This means you only need to set the styles for each element once. If you want to update the style of your website, you only need to do it in one place.

Imported CSS

You can use the @import rule to import rules from other style sheets.

Add either of the following between the <head>... </head> tags of all HTML documents that you want to import a style sheet into.

There is a great tutorial online for more information on CSS Class and much more on CSS than I am sharing here with you.
http://www.quackit.com/css/tutorial/css_class.cfm

STEP 3

Web Hosting (covered in chapter 6)

STEP 4

LEARN ABOUT WEB GRAPHICS

Web Graphics - Properties

Most browsers provide you with an easy way to view the properties of any graphic on the web. The following example demonstrates how to do this using Firefox on a Windows computer:

1. Load a web page with a graphic
2. Right click on the graphic, and select "Properties"

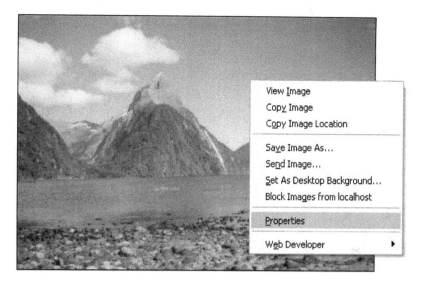

☐ You should now see the properties of the image:

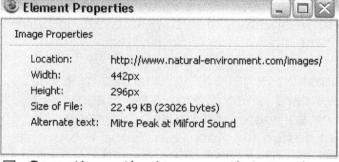

☐ Sometimes the image path is too long to fit in the window. In this case, depending on your browser, you may be able to click and drag the window to make it wider.

Displaying Web Graphics

Once an image has been created, it needs to be uploaded to a web server so that you can display it in your web pages. These are the steps you need to take in order to get a graphic to display on your website:

1. Create the graphic
2. Save it in a web format
3. Upload it to a web server
4. Embed the graphic into your web page (using HTML or CSS)
5. If you want to create graphics for your web page you'll need some form of graphics software. Depending on the graphic you need to create, you will need either *illustration* software or *image manipulation* software, or both.
6. An image manipulation program (also referred to as a "photo editor"), is normally used to modify existing images. It can also be used to create images, but there are some types of images that are much easier to create using illustration software. Image manipulation software is perfect for touching up and resizing photos.

Adobe Photoshop is generally regarded as the industry standard when it comes to image manipulation software and is used by many professional design studios. Paint Shop Pro is also another popular package.

7. If you'd prefer free software, try GIMP. GIMP is a great graphics package and is similar to Photoshop. The examples in this tutorial use GIMP.

    To learn more about GIMP, check out the GIMP tutorial.

8. Illustration software is normally used for creating illustration style images. Examples include logos, icons, decorative images, and illustrations.

9. Adobe Illustrator is a leading illustration package used by professional design studios around the world. Xara Xtreme is another popular package.
10. If you don't have the money to pay for a program like Illustrator or Xara Xtreme, try DrawPlus by FreeSerifSoftware. DrawPlus is free as long as it's for your own personal use.

Vector versus Pixel Based Software

11. Probably the biggest difference between illustration software and photo editing software is that one is *vector* based and the other is *pixel* based.
12. Illustration software is vector based. Without going into the technical details, one benefit you get from this is that you can scale your images up without the image deteriorating. With pixel based images, if you increase the size of the image, it gets all "pixelated". You may have seen this happen occasionally with images - it becomes blurry and the lines tend to look quite jagged.
13. Pixel based software (i.e. photo editors) also have their benefits. In particular, photo editors enable you to do some amazing things with photos. You can zoom right in and change colors pixel by pixel - something you can't do easily with vector based software.

Which One?

14. You may only need to use one of the two types of graphics software. This will depend on what type of graphic you need on your website. If you only want to touch up or resize photos, download GIMP. If you want to create a logo, or some sort

of illustration, download DrawPlus. If you're not sure, why not try them out anyway. That way, you'll get to see the different options that each one offers.

If you want to go into design, photo editing logos and much more on pictures than what I have covered here I recommend you go to:
http://www.quackit.com/web_graphics/tutorial/photo_editors.cfm

STEP 5
Learning JAVA Script

If you're new to programming/scripting, JavaScript is a good place to start. Having said that, it's still quite different to HTML so I recommend you take your time and cover off a little bit each day. Don't worry if it takes you several days to complete - it's better to fully understand everything than to brush over it and not fully comprehend it.

I suggest you bookmark this tutorial now, then continue on.

What is JavaScript?

JavaScript is a scripting language that enables web developers/designers to build more functional and interactive websites.

Common uses of JavaScript include:

- Alert messages

- Popup windows
- Dynamic dropdown menus
- Form validation
- Displaying date/time

JavaScript usually runs on the *client-side* (the browser's side), as opposed to *server-side* (on the web server). One benefit of doing this is performance. On the client side, JavaScript is loaded into the browser and can run as soon as it is called. Without running on the client side, the page would need to refresh each time you needed a script to run.

What do I need to create JavaScript?

You can create JavaScript using the same equipment you use when creating HTML. That is:

- Computer
- Text editor. For example, Notepad (for Windows), Pico (for Linux), or Simpletext (Mac). You could use a HTML editor if you like but it's not needed.
- Web Browser. For example, Internet Explorer or Firefox. You will need to ensure JavaScript is enabled within your browser's settings (this is normally enabled by default).

STEP 6
Cold Fusion

What Is ColdFusion?

ColdFusion is one of the easiest programming environments to use, and enables you to create powerful server-side web applications very quickly, with much less code than other technologies such as ASP, PHP etc.

ColdFusion integrates many Internet technologies such as XML, Java, web services etc, and as such, your applications can be as small or complex as required.

ColdFusion consists of two main elements:

- A ColdFusion server (which runs on top of your web server),
- ColdFusion templates (or files), which you write using ColdFusion Markup Language (CFML).

That's probably a very simplistic way of putting it, as there are many elements that make up a ColdFusion environment, but these two are essential if you want to build a ColdFusion application/website.

What Can ColdFusion Do?

ColdFusion enables you to build large, complex, and dynamic websites. ColdFusion can also increase your productivity enormously, both in development time and maintenance time.

With ColdFusion, you can build websites that do things such as:

- Query a database
- Allow users to upload files
- Create/read files on the server (for example, the files that your users upload)
- Have a "member's area" (i.e. via a login page)
- Have a shopping cart
- Present a customized experience (for example, based on users' browsing history)
- Create a "member's area" (i.e. via a login page)
- Send emails (for example, newsletters to a mailing list)
- Schedule tasks to run automatically (for example, your email newsletters)
- FTP files to/from another server
- Publish web services
- Much, much more

OK, I'm Sold. How Do I Get Started?

To build ColdFusion applications, you first need to install the ColdFusion server. Don't worry if that sounds like too much work - it's very straight forward. Installing ColdFusion is just like installing any other piece of software - you simply click your way through the installation wizard, configuring it as you go. This tutorial will point you in the right direction.

Once you've installed ColdFusion server, you can write code using the ColdFusion Markup Language (CFML). CFML uses a syntax that closely resembles HTML and XML. This makes it easy to learn if you're familiar with HTML or XML. CFML however, is more powerful than HTML - it is basically a programming language. You can write conditional statements, loops, query a database, send bulk emails, publish web services and much more.

ColdFusion also provides an administration interface (the ColdFusion Administrator), which enables you to customize your ColdFusion environment.

STEP 7
Learning about DataBase

A database is a collection of data. That may sound overly simplistic but it pretty much sums up what any database is.

A database could be as simple as a text file with a list of names. Or it could be as complex as a large, relational database management system, complete with in-built tools to help you maintain the data.

Before we get into dedicated database management systems, let's start with the basics - let's look at a simple text file example.

Text File

Imagine we have a text file called "Individual.txt", and that the contents look like this:

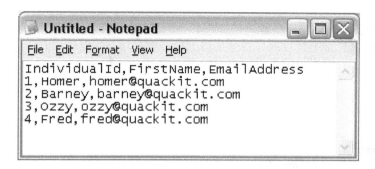

We could use this information to do things such as send an email to everyone on our list. We could do this because, due to the way we designed the list, we know that each *row* contains a different individual, and the information on that row is related to that individual. Also, the items in each row are separated by commas. Therefore, we know that the email address next to "Homer" is his email address. We could also call each row a *record*. Therefore, we currently have 4 records in our database.

With a small list like this, a text file may serve our purposes perfectly.

Spreadsheet

Another option would be to store it in a spreadsheet using spreadsheet software (for example, Microsoft Excel). That way, we could do some extra things with our list (such as format it, or sort by first name/surname etc).

A spreadsheet program like Excel makes these tasks relatively easy to do. Also, programs like Excel organize the data into *rows* and *columns*, making your data easier to comprehend. Something like this:

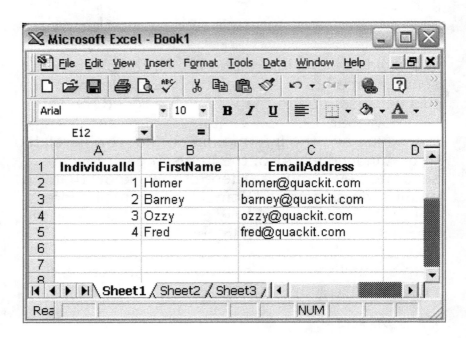

Database Software

A better option would be to store the data in a database *table* using specialized database software, such as Microsoft Access. Something like this:

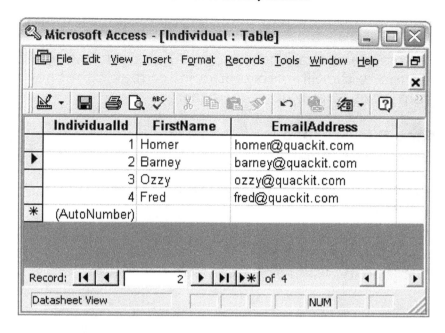

So What's the Difference?

You may be wondering what the difference is between the last two examples (Excel vs Access). After all, both examples have the data organized into rows and columns.

The differences between the 2 are many but the main thing here is to get you using a Database System of some kind. Access is great for home or for a small office use, otherwise to create a database driven website you are better off using a more robust system such as SQL Server, Oracle or MySQL. Even if you do not have access to Microsoft you can still follow along. Now the last 2 steps I personally have not learned and are therefore not going to write too much about them here accept to tell you what they are and where you can go to get the up to date tutorials on them if you wish. Please note I have personally built over 300 websites and my limited knowledge of the whole process has been enough to get me to the all important point of making money from what I have done thus far.

Step 8 is SQL and the tutorial link is http://www.quackit.com/sql/tutorial/ then

STEP 9 is Learn PHP and the link for the tutorial on that is http://www.quackit.com/php/tutorial/

8 CHAPTER
MONETIZING YOUR WEBSITE

I know of over 28 ways to monetize a website but I will attempt to simplify what I do know here for you to get the most of my knowledge. There are Direct Ways of monetizing your website and indirect ways let's have a look at both.

I started out with PPC Advertising Networks, these are pay per click advertising, Google Adsense I think is the most popular and my list of popular CPC (cost per click) advertising networks are; Google Adsense, Yahoo! Publisher Network, BidVertiser, Chitika and Clicksor.

The profitability of PPC advertising depends on the general traffic levels of the website and, most importantly, on the click-through rate (CTR) and cost per click (CPC). The CTR depends on the design of the website. Ads placed abode the fold or blended with content, for instance, tend to get higher CTRs. The CPC, on the other hand, depends on the nice of the website. Mortgages, financial products and college education are examples of profitable niches (clicks worth a couple of dollars are not rare), while tech-related topics tend to receive a smaller CPC (sometimes as low as a couple of cents per click).

The source of the traffic can also affect the overall CTR rate. Organic traffic (the one that comes from search engines) tends to perform well because these visitors were already looking for something, and they tend to click on ads more often. Social media traffic, on the other hand, presents terribly low CTRs because these visitors are tech-savvy and they just ignore ads.

CPM Advertising networks are similar to PPC networks except you get paid according to the number of impressions (page views) that the ads displayed on your site will generate. CPM stands for Cost Per Mille and it refers to the cost for 1,000 impressions. So if one of my websites generates 100,000 page views monthly a $1 CPM, I therefore earn $100 per month. CPM rates vary from network to network and the position of the ad on your website. The closer you place the ad to the top of the page the higher the CPM, the bigger the font the higher the CPM. You can get as low as 10 cents and as high as $10 per 1000 impressions (sometimes more) If you have a website with high page views per visitor ratio then this is for you. Some of my popular CPM advertising networks are:
Casale Media, Burst Media, Value Click, Advertising.com, Tribal Fusion and Right Media

The next direct advertising medium I use is Direct Banner Advertising. Selling your own advertising space is one of the most lucrative monetization methods. There is no middle man for commissions. The most popular banner formats on my websites are 728x90 leaderboard, 120x600 skyscraper and the 125x125 square button. The only thing with direct banner advertising is that you need to have big audience to get qualified advertisers and this can take time to develop but is worthwhile. My popular networks here are Commission Junction, Linkshare,

Clickbank and Overstock.

My next direct form of monetizing my websites is Text Link Ads. After Google declared that sites selling text links without the nofollow tag would be penalized, this monetization method became less popular.

Many website owners are still using text links to monetize their sites, though, some using the nofollow tag and some not.

The advantage of this method is that it is not intrusive. One can sell text links directly through his website or use specialized networks like Text-Link-Ads and Text-Link-Brokers to automate the process.

Text link marketplaces and networks:

- DigitalPoint Link Sales Forum
- Text-Link-Ads
- Text-Link-Brokers
- TNX
- LinkWorth

The next way of direct monetizing my websites is through Affiliate Marketing and this is my favourite way. Under this system you have a merchant that is willing to let other people (the affiliates) sell directly or indirectly its products and services, in exchange for a commission. Sometimes this type of advertising is also called CPA (cost per action) or CPL (cost per lead) based.

Affiliates can send potential customers to the merchant using several tools, from banners to text links and product reviews.

In order to find suitable affiliate programs you can turn to individual companies and publishers like Dreamhost and SEOBook, or join affiliate marketplaces and networks.

List of popular affiliate marketplaces and networks:

- Commission Junction
- ClickBank
- Azoogle Ads
- Link Share
- Amazon

One of the latest trends from (June 2013) to monetize your websites direct is through Monetization Widgets. Examples include Widgetbucks and Smartlinks. Some of these services operate under the PPC scheme, others like text link ads whilst others leverage affiliate links. The main difference here is that they work as web widgets so you plug and play the service onto your website. So to find these go to WidgetBucks, ScratchBack or SmartLinks.

Another way is to direct monetize your website is to sponsor reviews. Joining one of these sponsored reviews marketplaces will give you the opportunity to write sponsored posts on a wide range of topics. Not all bloggers are willing to get paid to write about a specific product or website (because it might compromise the editorial credibility), but the ones who do are making good money out of it.

If your blog has a big audience you could also offer sponsored reviews directly, cutting off the commissions of the middleman.

List of sponsored reviews and paid blogging networks:

- PayPerPost
- Sponsored Reviews
- ReviewMe
- BlogVertise
- Smorty

The next method of monetizing your website can be with the new technology of RSS FEEDS. Millions of internet users and website owners are now finding ways to monetize this new content distribution channel. Feedburner already has its own publisher network and you can sign up to start displaying CPM based ads on your feed footer. So go to either Feedburner, BidVertiser or Pheedo.

Now if you have a website that has specific columns or events for example a weekly webinar, an interview series or something of that nature then have a look at Mashable which illustrates how you increase your income being the web owner while giving the advertisers the possibility to target a more specific audience with a reduced commitment. Problogger also runs group writing projects occasionally and before proceeding he publicly announces the project asking for sponsors.

As we all know while the Internet is populated with free forums, there is also the possibility to create a private one where members need to pay a single or recurring fee to join.

SEO Blackhat charges $100 monthly from its members, and they have thousands of them. Obviously in order to charge such a price for a forum membership you need to provide real value for the members (e.g., secret techniques, tools, and so on).

Performancing also launched a private forum recently, focused on the networking aspect. It is called The Hive, and the monthly cost is $10.

These are just two examples. There are many possibilities to create a private and profitable forum, you just need to find an appealing angle that will make it worth for the members.

List of popular forum software:

- vBulletin
- Simple Machines Forum
- phpBB
- Vanilla

The next enlightenment is Job Boards. All the popular blogs are trying to leverage job boards to make some extra income. Guy Kawasaki, ReadWriteWeb, Problogger... you name it.

Needless to say that in order to create an active and profitable job board you need first to have a blog focused on a specific niche, and a decent amount traffic.

The advantage of this method is that it is passive. Once you have the structure in place, the job listings will come naturally, and you can charge anywhere from $10 up to $100 for each.

List of popular job board software:

- JobThread
- Web Scribe Job Board
- SimplyHired Job-o-matic
- Jobbex

Not far from this example is the paid surveys and polls, basically there are services that will pay you money to run a small survey or poll on your website. The most popular one is called Vizu Answers.

Basically you need to sign up with them, and select the kind of polls that you want to run your site. Most of these services operate under a CPM model.

Alright now I have given you so many ways to direct monetize your websites let's now add a few indirect methods of making more money from your websites. One of the oldest money making strategies on the web is to promote an eBook related to your website. This is a very efficient way to generate revenue. You can structure the website around the eBook or launch the eBook based on the success of the website. Here is my popular list of links to assist to earn money from eBooks; Writing an ebook for your blog

How to sell ebooks

Processing payments for your ebook

How to sell digital products online

List of ebook selling software

Selling a Hardcover Book, recently as I am interested in this topic currently I have discovered many authors and journalists leverage their blogs or websites to sell copies of hardcover books. Examples include Guy Kawasaki, Seth Godin and Malcolm Gladwell.

While most of these people were already renowned authors before they created their website, one could also follow the other way around. Lorelle VanFossen did exactly that with her Blogging Tips book. First she built her authority on the subject via her blog, and afterwards she published the book.

List of self publishing and publishing services:

- Lulu
- Self Publishing
- iUniverse
- WordClay

You know we all have knowledge on some things and it is the ability to get this knowledge out there for others benefits that will earn you money. Depending on your niche, you could make money by offering consulting and related services. If you are also the author of your website, the development, the articles and information that you share will build a profile and certify your expertise on that niche, making it easier to gain customers.

For those of us who are very serious in making money through the internet and our websites then you also need to look at mentoring programs and creating a conference around your website. Now I know that sounds a bit out there but I have done both of these things and the journey there is yet another book!

9 CHAPTER
TRAFFIC AND CONVERSION TO MONEY

By now as we are getting closer to the end of this book, I have taught you many things. It is very true what my friend Tom Hua who I believe is the Godfather of the Internet says, You need 3 things to make money on the internet, you need a product that is in demand, you need a website as your tool to get your product out there to the marketplace and you need converting traffic. What does converting traffic mean? In this chapter I am going to try to simply state my journey and my understanding of this term.

If you do not have the visitors to your website then how can you possibly then keep them on your website long enough to make a sale? The use of great content, value for the person and ease of use all come into this, but it does come down to your original research of your term or your keyword rich title which will bring the visitor to your site but then to turn that visitor into a customer I see you need three more things. A product the visitor is looking for, 3 clicks from find to sell and this is where your ease of use for your website comes in and the 3rd thing is follow up – customer service. This is something that seems to have gone out the window today, and I know that if you give great customer service then you will have that customer come back again and again. So let's have a closer look at this.

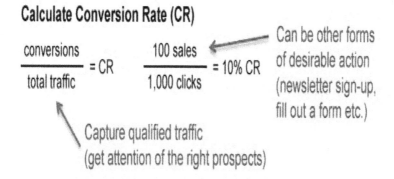

Calculate Conversion Rate (CR)

$$\frac{\text{conversions}}{\text{total traffic}} = CR \qquad \frac{100 \text{ sales}}{1,000 \text{ clicks}} = 10\% \text{ CR}$$

Can be other forms of desirable action (newsletter sign-up, fill out a form etc.)

Capture qualified traffic (get attention of the right prospects)

Calculate Return On Investment (ROI)

Revenue: 100 sales = $100

Cost: 1,000 clicks = $20

$$\frac{\text{Revenue}}{\text{Cost}} = ROI \qquad \frac{\$100}{\$20} = 5 \text{ ROI}$$

You don't want just any click, you want qualified prospects clicking on your links, visiting your website and consuming your content.

Let's be clear, getting attention is only part of the equation to help you increase conversions but it does not automatically equal to conversion.

For those of you who don't know why qualified traffic is important, let me just say that if you want to increase conversions of your landing page or your ecommerce store, this is crucial.

What is a Conversion?

How does the value of a conversion relate to the return on investment of a marketing campaign?

Basically a conversion is an action a user takes on your site that has value to your business.

Typically it's a sale but it can also be a newsletter sign-up, a download of a file, viewing of a video, or a request for more information.

If you know what a conversion is worth to you, and the percentage of traffic visiting your conversion page versus the traffic that do convert (the conversion rate), then it is easy to calculate your return on investment (ROI) for just about any marketing campaign.

From the calculations on the previous page, you may think that if you want to increase ROI, you just need to increase CR right?

You're on the right track but that's not the entire story here because conversion rates typically depend on two factors:

1. **Qualified traffic** – The goal is to capture only traffic that's more likely to convert. This is where direct marketing is heavily used to grab the attention of the visitors. A valuable piece of content, a paid search ad or recommendations from social media channels are just a few ways you can use to obtain qualified traffic.
2. **Landing page** – A landing page is a specific area of your website where traffic is sent (via links from online advertisements, organic search results, social media or email) specifically to prompt a certain action or result. And since a visitor usually lands on a page

after clicking on a link, it's important that the links you use to send traffic to your website is relevant to what that person is looking for. Once on your landing page, it's basically a tactic of one-on-one selling so if it's not what people are looking for, you will likely get a low conversion.

There are tons of strategies to get qualified traffic (paid search, SEO, email, display, affiliate, etc.), but today we're going to look at things that you can do to your website to help you improve your conversion rate.

These tips are easy to implement and can start improving your results immediately. You need to ask the following questions and even create a scorecard if you wish on each of your websites. Please note these are just some of my recommendations that once I implemented them I got more targeted traffic to my sites.

These questions are all for your landing page of your website;

- **Is the target audience well defined?**
- **Does the user experience what the target is looking for?**
- **Is the value proposition or USP (unique selling proposition) clear?**
- **Is the content optimized for online reading?**
- **Does the site copy clearly answer the 5 Ws, (who what where when why) and 1 H question (How)?**
- **Do the images and videos support the value propositions?**

- **Is the content properly anchored with the keywords you want to rank for?**
- **Are you doing any tests that will yield insights to higher conversions?**
- **Are you tracking web analytics that's relevant to your conversions?**

If you score each answer to these questions from 1-5 for 1 Poor 2 Fair 3 Passable 4 Good 5 Excellent

Then add them up:

9-15 Poor

16-25 Fair

26-35 Passable

36-45 Good

46-55 Excellent

By conducting this very simple audit on your landing page you can improve your qualified traffic to your landing page overall by 70% plus.

The most important thing that you can do to increase your conversion rate is to know who you're targeting and tailor your content for that person.

When a new visitor lands on your site for the first time and clicks on a link or goes to your product page, and doesn't buy anything (or fill out a lead form), then you've probably lost them for good.

A landing page is tailored to fit the specific call?to?action (that you designated) and is often the first page a visitor sees when clicking on a link. The challenge is to ensure that you are optimizing an exceptional online experience for visitors and also producing high ROI.

So what is considered an exceptional online experience?

It's basically providing visitors with accurate, relevant and useful information to meet their needs. But do it in an entertaining and engaging way to differentiate yourself.

None of the bait-and-switch tactics or hype that's overpromised and under-delivered. A positive user experience usually focuses on a single message with a strong call-to-action that are written in plain language with no more than 7-12 words.

Don't make the mistake of trying to combine all the features and benefits of your offer, instead focus on the highest value outcome.

Once you have a clean and precise message, you can make it credible with branding elements such as logos and security icons (third-party verifications) or use stories and testimonials. This will give confidence to the visitor which can have a positive impact on conversion as well.

Perfecting, or at the very least improving, customer experience has replaced customer loyalty as the ultimate corporate PR and brand reputation.

Put yourself in your visitor's shoes and ask: would I scroll down and read this?

Would I fill out this form and give my personal information?

Why would I click here?

A value proposition is basically your offer. What are the main selling points? Why should the visitor buy right there and then? It may sound obvious to you but a clear value proposition is the foundation to your conversions.

Your landing page should address the top questions and concerns prospects have about your offer. And it usually goes back to the four Ps of marketing: product, price, place and promotion.

Too often, internet marketers focus too much on "promotion" instead of combining the other three Ps.

You may find after studying the competition that increasing or decreasing your price is likely to result in better conversions, for example. Perhaps there is a distribution channel, such as the social networks or email marketing; you haven't fully integrated into your marketing mix.

And with products, developing a new product or re-package an existing product may provide a lift to your overall conversion as well.

You are likely to increase the chance of conversion if you have a clear value proposition that pushes the visitor to take action with your offer.

Ask yourself whether your landing page is helping people to make their decision.

If it's not, then why should people do what you ask of them? (Purchase a product, sign up for newsletter or request a demo...etc.)

Don't forget to research your competition so you know how your value proposition stacks up.

The new consumer-led digital revolution is all about exceeding customers' expectations via influence.

Simply put, influence is conversion rate. So you make a difference by your web content, presentation etc and the visitor will become a customer = $$$

Create Compelling Copy with Clear Headlines

The first things a visitor reads after landing on your page is your headline. This is when you need to pass the smell test.

If your headline is anything less than clear, informative and compelling, you will bore or confuse your visitors into leaving.

On the other hand, a well-written headline can drive your visitors to take a closer look even if it's just text.

Have you noticed how some landing pages are super long?

These landing pages are called "long-form" sales letter that typically consists of a title, subtitle, bunch of paragraphs, images, testimonials and a few buy buttons on a plain-looking page that you have to scroll on and on.

Think about it, if it doesn't convert well why would there be so many long-form landing pages online?

The truth is people only read what they're interested in even if it appears to be too long!

The key is to do so in an engaging way that will connect with your audience, it can even be fun and entertaining.

One of my ways to start creating engaging copy is to use the five W's and one H technique. Here is an example of this:

- Tell them why they're about to read the page
- Tell them who's it for
- Tell them what's in it for them
- Tell them where they're at or where they can get it
- Tell them when they can get it (i.e. limited time offer)
- Tell them how it works or how it relates to them

The goal is to focus on everything you think will push them one step closer to taking your converting and nothing more. Make sure you get to the point with actionable content (tell them what to do next) that focuses more on the outcome rather than the feature. In the last chapter i gave you the questions to ask and how you can rate your landing page so now this expands on that table even more.

When using images and videos, ask yourself whether that piece of content is drawing attention away from your persuasive message or adding to it.

10 CHAPTER
RENOVATION AND KEEPING UP

Have you ever renovated a house? Have you ever built an addition to a house? Have you ever had a new house built and moved in? No you are not now reading a book on house building but I needed to give you an analogy for renovating your website. Same as for a house, there are always changes no matter what scenario for your house and I need you to look at your website the same way. You need to keep your website current, eye catching, alive and make sure it always has your customer in mind and the final value give, give, give.
Then and only then will you attract visitors who then become customers hence converting into sales.

One of the ways I try to keep up to date is to do testing on my landing pages of my websites. The golden rule of any direct response marketing is to ensure you evoke a measurable, tractable response.

This means constant testing of your landing page using methods such as a/b split testing or multivariate testing.

The concept is simple.

You want to have variations of the page to be tested on an ongoing basis so you can improve conversion rate.

- **What is an A/B split test?** A classic direct marketing tactic, A/B testing is a method of marketing testing by which a baseline control sample is compared to a variety of single-variable test samples in order to improve response rates It's typically performed to determine the better of two content variations

- **What is a multivariate test?**
  A slightly more complex test, multivariate test is a process by which more than one component of a website may be tested in a live environment. It can be thought of in simple terms as numerous A/B tests performed on one page at the same time.

By conducting tests on your landing page, you will be able to determine which headline is more effective or what layout works better.

Here is an example case of an A/B split test that I did on my email marketing.

The objective was to determine if removing the sidebar would result in a better overall performance. I also tested two different email subject line to see which one opens better.

Sidebar vs. No Sidebar with Different Headline

Open rate: 47%
Click rate: 16%
CR: 1.4%

Open rate: 40%
Click rate: 15%
CR: 2.9%

2X Conversion Rate!

The obvious winner here is the control version. The result indicated that the new version (without sidebar) has a higher open rate compare to the control version (email with sidebar), but the conversion rate was substantially lower.

Keep in mind that with testing you want to make sure you gather enough data (sample size) to ensure that your tests are statistically relevant. Sounds complicated? Well, thanks to Google, you can use their Website Optimizer to conduct both of these tests for free! So when it comes to testing and keeping up to date here are some ideas you can use:

- **Test different headlines, sub headlines and ad copy**
- **Test different version of the same logo, icons, layout of testimonials and even colors**
- **Test different call-to-actions and buttons (i.e. try this vs. buy now)**
- **Test different images or videos (swap image for video and vice versa)**
- **Test different forms (embed in different areas of the site, reduce required fields)**
- **Test different offers (use incentives to see how discounts or coupons work differently)**
- **Test long versus short sales page**

Part of this also is to keep track of everything you do and the best way I do this is through Google analytics- this is an invaluable tool which is totally FREE. By using Google Analytics you will know the sources that deliver traffic to your landing pages from pay-per-click (PPC), email marketing, social media, organic searches or even offline advertising channels.

Knowing the source of your most profitable traffic is the key to increase ROI. (Return On Investment)

The more detail you get with where traffic comes and goes the more clear you will see how visitors reacts to your offer.

There are many ways to aggregate your website data from Google Analytics but if you want to focus on conversion rate, start by looking at the following areas (just to name a few):

- **Traffic source** – where are people coming from? This is your channel acquisition strategy.
- **Visitor loyalty** – How long do people stay? How many pages do they visit and how many times do they visit between two or more times.
- **Bounce rate** – How relevant is your landing page? Bounce rate measures the percentage of single-page visits or visits in which the person left your site from where they landed on. The more relevant your landing pages, the more visitors will stay on your site and convert
- **Keywords** – This shows you what queries (keywords) are mapped to your landing pages that sends you traffic. This is a good indicator of what keywords your website is ranked for and how search engines interpret your content.

Last but not least, listen and learn from your customers to make sure what you're tracking matches to the story your data is telling you.

It's as easy as picking up the phone and call the customers yourself!

If you aren't able to do that, try conducting regular online surveys or implement some type of post-sale customer feedback system.

The Take Away

In the era of engagement, consumers no longer separate marketing between in-store or online experience—it is the experience.

Whether you're making a sale in person or receiving a conversion online, conversion rate is the vote of confidence that creates personal relationships.

It is trust, likability, authority and ultimately, influence.

Nothing prevents you from trying to increase your conversion rate. If you do nothing, your conversion rate will normalize over time (stays the same).

However; while conversion is an important factor to the profitability of your marketing, you shouldn't lose sight on the big picture – that's building your brand equity.

When you have brand equity, you have top-of-mind recalls.

This means you command attention and your message will have a higher chance of cutting through the noise of the increasing irrelevant landscape of "push" advertising. Influence will convert visitors into customers time and again.

When I am taking a critical look at my website apart from the testing and tracking I also look at the theme used, the plugins are current and up to date and the cache is removed. I also have as much in place to stop or at the very least reduce spam.

I use Akismet and also Wordfense Security plugins in order to assist in this and WP-supercache to remove cache, all of this done regularly does assist in keeping your website scroll evenly and stay quick to open up and move between links and pages.

In summary I believe I have written a great 'road map' to anyone being able to start their own business online that not only will be successful but once set up properly will be a passive income for as long as you wish.

According to a recent study by Morgan Stanley, online marketing is a $50 billion opportunity simply because eyeballs are moving online.

People spend more and more time online, and the ad dollars just follow people to the web.

This is where the change is happening.

People need information to find jobs, solve problems, buy products, get dates, seek professional advice, and they want to do it in the fastest and easiest way possible – via the Internet.

Everyone is searching for solutions to their problems on the Internet, and this is where you can come in to bridge the gap In a paradigm shift like this you can defy conventional wisdom to break into new markets without having to fight for competitive advantage, battle over market share, and struggle for differentiation.

Be yourself and just as Confucius was the first one to say, "choose a job you love and you will never have to work a day in your life."

Working hard is simply not enough.

When it comes to building your own business, the hardest part is building momentum and realizing that you must invest in yourself, take action, and continue to learn.

One of the things everyone talks about as part of keeping your website up to date is the use of Social Media. Almost every article you come across on the web has a sharing option to either Tweet it or to post it on your Facebook wall. This is a great way to build awareness about your website's products or services. In addition, search engines like Google are using social elements to determine the relevancy of your content. The more your content is shared, the more valuable it is perceived by search engines and this will gain you more ranking points. Adding sharing buttons on your website has never been easier. There are free widgets across the web that give you the code needed to display the share buttons on your site or blog. Some even tell you where to place the code on your web page. By having share buttons on your website and blog, you make it easy for visitors to share your content right within your website without having to navigate to social networks. It is well-known that people are more likely to listen to their friends' recommendations than to what an expert in the field might say. By not allowing sharing on your website, you are missing out being recommended by your visitors.

Another component of your website is video, either you make the video yourself or search to find the relevant video for your website. The closest thing to real life on the web today is video. By incorporating video into your website, you add that extra touch of reality that your visitors can connect with. About 60 hours of video are uploaded on YouTube every minute. You can decide to either tap from this huge online resource or take your own videos using a Smartphone or a Flip video camera. You can start with a welcome video that tells your visitors what you do and what your business is all about right on the homepage. Your blog can also feature video posts where you post talking heads interviews or your own testimonials. Videos that feature industry thought leaders and 'how-to' content are particularly popular online and can help boost your website as a valuable resource for information.

Frequent updates are crucial for your website and without them the website is just a dusty archive of outdated posts. Such website could harm your good name so the improvement should not be too delayed.
Your Website is a form of communication - a visitors communicate with you by visiting your website. Outdated and obsolete articles will convince them that you do not wish to communicate with them. So update your content at least twice a month. Imagine a customer trying to buy a product and only due to lack of websites updates he buys a discounted product, which is neither discounted anymore, nor offered.

Not only will that customer never buy anything else on the same website, but he/she will most likely share that bad experience with others. And the number of customers who most likely will not make any further purchase increase exponentially. E-shops require continuous and very frequent care – particularly that depends on the type and turnover of the goods and many other factors.

Efficiency, reliability and transparency of the website should be your aim. More updated websites have generally higher attendance. Every change you create should be displayed on the website immediately. Keep in mind that customers need to reach easily the contact information, newest prices, products and catalogues. Discussions demand frequent care – although visitors mostly share their experience, the admin should take part in the discussion and respond flexibly to requests, suggestions or complaints. Some outdated elements might even be awkward. For example „Joke of the day" which has been posted months ago seems ridiculous rather than funny.

When it comes to managing the websites content you must keep in mind that less is more. So updating does not only mean addition of new information, but removal of the old one as well. This might seem obvious but even a little mistake can make an unpleasant consequence. Whether we talk about outdated sales and campaigns mentioned above or just about dead links. The customer needs to be informed but not overwhelmed by information. If you need to insert many new articles and you wish to keep the old ones, you should create a special archive and enable the visitors to search in the content of the website.

In a nutshell, websites updates matters. The correct functioning of the website depends on the updates and maintenance. On the Internet can be found many companies offering the websites maintenance as a paid service. Despite this fact it depends on your decision if you choose to take care of the website on your own, or you prefer others to do it for you. And if you decide to be the one, do not forget to backup every previous version of your web.

Alright so to summarize I have a 6 step guide to finally assist you in keeping up to date with all the latest and greatest.

1. Check Your Copyright Date - Nothing signals out-of-date faster than scrolling down a home page and seeing Copyright 2002, when it is 2011. The visitor instantly wonders what else is out of date. Instead, set a calendar reminder for yourself at the beginning of each year to go in and update the copyright/date.

2. Update Your Press Section - The news or press section of your website isn't only used by members of the media. Potential customers visit press sections to get an understanding of a company's credibility. If you haven't posted a news announcement in months or even a year, then your press page turns into a liability, rather than an asset. To fix this, do not include the date next to your news announcements. This is merely a band-aid. A better solution is to make public relations part of your marketing mix and consider using a social media newsroom to make your media page a credible asset for customer acquisition.

3. Blog Consistently - Have a blog? Great. Haven't blogged in six months? Not Great. Having a blog is a major part of successful inbound marketing. It is important that you commit to creating content consistently. Understand that it is less about frequency and more about consistency. While publishing once or more a week is best, once a month is also great providing that you post every month at the same general time. This will set the right expectations with your subscribers and make your blog look credible to new visitors.

4. Avoid "New" - Using the word "new" especially as it refers to products, can be an invitation to having a dated website. The problem with saying that something is new, is that many businesses don't take the time to remove the "new" once the product has been out on the market for an extended period of time. Instead, it is better to create a featured products sections that can include both new and important/products.

5. Keep Contact Information Current - This might seem like a simple one, but it happens far too often. Having a phone number, fax number or even an address that is not current is a guaranteed way to lose prospects. If someone calls a number that no longer works, they will instantly question your business and wonder if your business is still in operation. Whenever you perform a business operations change, make sure to check if a website change needs to happen as well.

6. Incorporate Relevant Widgets For Dynamic Content - Every business has busy times and slower times. If you are in a time where you can't create as much content as you would like to, or don't have a new product announcement looming, you can still show that your website is a "living-and-breathing" part of your business. One way to do this is by using widgets to provide fresh content automatically for website visitors. This could be a Facebook widget that shows the most recent comments on your business page or maybe it is a Twitter widget that shows the most recent messages from industry experts. This content can really be anything as long as it is valuable to your customers and prospects. No matter what type of website you own, the goal is most likely to get people to visit it. A website with traffic can form communities, make money, and increase your reputation online. Getting traffic to your website is important, but getting those people to come back to your website more than once is of the utmost importance. The best way to do this is to keep your website up-to-date.

Nothing screams, "worthless website!" louder than broken links and out-of-date information. Broken links are links that point to places that no longer exist or are out of date. Check these frequently to avoid embarrassment and to prevent loss of website visitor confidence. You can do this by clicking on every link, or use an online service that performs the task for you. Likewise, make sure the information contained in your website - or the links it points to - is up-to-date. Sharing news from two years ago is not a good idea.

Keeping your website up-to-date is important for both internet business owners and personal website owners. If you want to entertain and inform your visitors, and encourage them to come back again and again, you must update regularly. Write new blog posts and give them more information, a new anecdote, or a graphic to view. Let them know what is coming up with news and announcements. And never scare them away by keeping old information and links active on your website.

It seems strange to me to have finally finished writing this book. It has taken me over a year to write and I have enjoyed it immensely. I really do love the internet and the potential income people can make by using the internet as a tool to make money. You all have the tools in hand now to assist you in making a difference in your life financially and therefore give you the freedom to live out your life without having the worry of money.

My mentors have made my internet world a lot clearer and I hope in any small way this book can do the same for you.

APPENDIX OF USEFUL WEBSITE LINKS

http://googleeasysearch.com

http://youtu.be/cuYwP47qC1I Searching for a term referred to from page 9 chapter 2.

http://youtu.be/z50WY52FAug Creating a customized Facebook Page this is on page 11 Chapter 2

http://youtu.be/1SinIE9q9Ig Creating a link on your website for your customized Facebook Page, this is on page 11 chapter 2

http://youtu.be/katEI9eAY4I finding a hot product through ebay Page 11 Chapter 2

http://youtu.be/e-Jcp8tnchI Creating a link to your website

https://www.google.com/adsense you will need to copy and paste this link into your browser to get it to work. Chapter 4 page 16.

http://www.roboform.com page 17 Chapter 4

https://affiliate-program.amazon.com page 18
Chapter 4

http://www.cj.com/get-started-now page 19
chapter 4

http://tinyurl.com/bvpwrhg this is the link to
Chitika page 20 Chapter 4

http://wordpress.org Chapter 6 Page 30

www.blogger.com www.wordpress.com both of these
links are on page 38 Chapter 7

. www.wix.com page 38 Chapter 7

www.webstarts.com page 38 Chapter 7

www.weebly.com page 38 Chapter 7

www.webspawner.com page 38 Chapter 7

www.jigsy.com page 38 Chapter 7

www.webs.com page 39 Chapter 7

www.judijaques.com page 40 chapter 7

http://www.quackit.com/css/tutorial/css_class.cfm
page 51 Chapter 7

http://www.quackit.com/web_graphics/tutorial/phot
o_editors.cfm   page 55 chapter 7

http://www.quackit.com/sql/tutorial/ then **STEP 9
is Learn PHP** and the link for the tutorial on that is

http://www.quackit.com/php/tutorial/ page 63
chapter 7

http://brettmcfall.com

http://stevenessa.com

LIST OF VALUE ADD ON'S

Need some extra help? I run a program called

F.A.S.T Affiliate Sustainable Training which consists of 7 DVD's which because you have a copy of my book is at a valued price of $197

If that is not enough as the one on one tutoring is not included with the DVD's then I have a membership website that does give you all the extra one on one videos and contacts. You can become a member for Free for one month, try the system out then after that there are monthly fee structures to suit all budgets.

To have a one on one hour with me the consulting charge is $500 per hour.

Again as you have a copy of this book it entitles you to FREE entry to any ONE of my live seminars anywhere I am appearing.

The last value add for you is a complete done for you website complete with 5 affiliate memberships. Total cost $2000 but reduced to $1000 because you have a copy of my book.

CONDITIONS

To claim any of the offers you must have your copy of my book with you on entry to an event or you must mention this page and place of purchase to claim your choice from the above list.

http://judijaques.com

f.a.s.t
Technology
Consulting

ABOUT THE AUTHOR

Judi
Jaques

All books come to an end but it has been pointed out to me that I need to tell you a bit about me. Let me just say I have come from humble beginnings. I have been with my one and only husband for 40 years, we had 2 amazing children and currently 5 grandchildren. I was a registered nurse for 30 years and achieved 3 degrees in nursing. 13 years ago I left nursing and started my own business, a tourism business. Today this is still running as a very successful business. I have always been drawn to the internet both in my nursing life and business life and formerly started my own second business in 2010. This is a complete online business, after paying for serious mentorship I have now appeared on many stages here in Australia. I love people and showing people my affiliate ways is a lot of fun. I will continue my quest as the internet changes all the time. I will not stop until my working model of having 5 independent internet arms all earning $10,000 per month, every month! My gain- freedom, time and the ability to help a lot more people financially. If you would like to join me on this journey-

Live events are always fun, exciting and incredible value! My list of appearances can be found on my website http://judijaques.com